anythink

RECYCLING MATERIALS

By Gemma McMullen

KidHaven
PUBLISHING

Published in 2017 by
KidHaven Publishing, an Imprint of Greenhaven Publishing, LLC
353 3rd Avenue
Suite 255
New York, NY 10010

© 2017 Booklife Publishing
This edition is published by arrangement with Booklife Publishing

Designer: Drue Rintoul
Editor: Gemma McMullen

Cataloging-in-Publication Data

Names: McMullen, Gemma.
Title: Recycling materials / Gemma McMullen.
Description: New York : KidHaven Publishing, 2017. | Series: Environmental issues | Includes index.
Identifiers: ISBN 9781534520493 (pbk.) | ISBN 9781534520516 (library bound) | ISBN 9781534520509 (6 pack) | ISBN 9781534520523 (ebook)
Subjects: LCSH: Recycling (Waste, etc.)–Juvenile literature.
Classification: LCC TD794.5 M36 2017 | DDC 363.72'82–dc23

Printed in the United States of America

CPSIA compliance information: Batch #CW17KL: For further information contact Greenhaven Publishing LLC, New York, New York at 1-844-317-7404.

Please visit our website, www.greenhavenpublishing.com. For a free color catalog of all our high-quality books, call toll free 1-844-317-7404 or fax 1-844-317-7405.

Photo Credits: Abbreviations: l–left, r–right, b–bottom, t–top, c–center, m–middle.
All images are courtesy of Shutterstock.com.

Front Cover - monticello. 1 - monticello. 2 - Evan Lorne. 3t - donikz. 3m - Somchai Som. 3b - SeDmi. 4 - Roy Pedersen. 5 - Dmitry Kalinovsky. 6 - Paradise On Earth. 7inset - Sergiy Bykhunenko. 7b - e X p o s e. 8 - auremar. 9 - luis abrantes. 9inset - Kenneth William Caleno. 10 - absolutimages. 11 - kryzhov. 11inset - LI CHAOSHU. 12 - RTimages. 13 - thechatat. 14 - bioraven. 15 - Joseph Sohm. 16 - kao. 16inset - Andrey N Bannov. 17 - tobkatrina. 17inset - Alan Bailey. 18 - mtsyri. 18inset - EloPaint. 19 - Jack Frog. 20 - Lightspring. 21 - bluedogroom. 21inset - Velychko. 22l - Zuzule. 22r - Patricia Hofmeester. 23l - Monkey Business Images. 23r - charles taylor. 24 - absolutimages.

CONTENTS

Words in **bold** can be found in the Glossary on page 24.

WHAT IS GARBAGE?

Garbage is made up of the things that we no longer want or need. We each create a large amount of garbage every day.

Every year, the world produces more than 2 billion tons of waste!

Our garbage is taken away using special trucks. Garbage is either buried or burned, neither of which is very good for the **environment**.

REDUCE, REUSE, RECYCLE!

By reducing the amount of garbage that we create, we can help the environment. We can reuse items, rather than throwing them away.

THIS EMPTY JAR IS BEING USED AS A PENCIL HOLDER.

Recycling is when we turn old products into new ones.

THESE CHILDREN ARE USING UNWANTED COOKING TOOLS TO PLAY.

CAN YOU TELL WHAT THESE CHAIRS USED TO BE?

7

WHAT CAN BE RECYCLED?

Many household items can be recycled. Paper, plastic, glass, and metal can all be recycled. In most areas, these materials are collected from each house.

THIS SYMBOL IS SHOWN WHEN SOMETHING IS SUITABLE FOR RECYCLING.

The materials are taken away and sorted into groups.

CLEAR GLASS
Bottles & Jars only

GREEN GLASS
Bottles & Jars only

UNWANTED GOODS

THERE ARE ALSO RECYCLING CENTERS WHERE UNWANTED GOODS CAN BE TAKEN.

RECYCLING PAPER

Paper can be recycled. At the recycling center, the paper is separated into different types. A soapy liquid is used to remove any ink from the paper.

Did you know that we throw away enough wood and paper each year to heat 50,000 homes for 20 years?

Water is added to the paper to make a **slurry**. The slurry is spread out and left to dry.

THIS TOILET PAPER WAS MADE USING RECYCLED PAPER.

RECYCLING PLASTIC

There are many different types of plastic. Most plastics can be recycled. Once the different types of plastics have been separated, the plastic is melted down.

Did you know that some plastics can take up to 500 years to **decompose**?

The plastic can then be **remolded** into a new shape and used again.

THIS TABLE WAS MADE FROM RECYCLED PLASTIC.

13

RECYCLING GLASS

Glass can be recycled. At the recycling center, the glass is grouped by color. The glass is then washed to remove any germs.

CLEAR

GREEN

BROWN

The clean glass is crushed and melted before it is remolded. Glass can be recycled over and over again.

GLASS KEEPS ITS COLOR EVEN AFTER IT IS MELTED.

RECYCLING METAL

Some metals can be recycled. Like plastic and glass, they are sorted, washed, and melted before being reshaped.

Steel and aluminium are types of metal that can be recycled. Most of our food and drink cans are made of steel or aluminium.

Did you know that powerful magnets are used to sort through different types of metals?

RECYCLING TEXTILES

A textile is any item made from cloth or an **artificial** fabric such as vinyl. Textiles are used for clothing, linens, bedding, upholstery, curtains, carpets, and other items. Any textile item, even if it is worn, torn, or stained, can be recycled!

The fabrics are grouped by color. They are then **shredded** into tiny fibers and **blended** with other fibers before being made into new fabric.

THIS TOWEL IS MADE FROM RECYCLED FABRIC.

19

RECYCLING GREEN WASTE

Green waste is a mixture of grass and leaves from the garden, as well as fruit and vegetable scraps. Green waste can be used as compost.

Compost is used in soil in the garden. Compost has many nutrients in it and helps new plants grow.

WHAT ELSE CAN BE REUSED OR RECYCLED?

Collected rainwater can be used to water plants during periods of dry weather.

Reusable diapers are much better for the environment.

This tire makes a fun swing!

Try giving unwanted toys to a friend rather than throwing them out!

GLOSSARY

artificial not natural
blended mixed with another material
decompose to break down naturally
environment the natural world
remolded reshaped
shredded cut into very small pieces
slurry a mixture that is partly liquid

INDEX